AN AUGMENTED REALITY
SCIENCE EXPERIENCE

CURIOUS PEARL
INVESTIGATES LIGHT

by Eric Braun

illustrated by Stephanie Dehennin

PICTURE WINDOW BOOKS
a capstone imprint

Curious Pearl here! Do you like science?
I sure do! I have all sorts of fun tools to help
me observe and investigate, but my favorite tool
is my science notebook. That's where I write
down questions and facts that help me learn
more about science. Would you like to
join me on my science adventures?
You're in for a special surprise!

Download the Capstone 4D app!

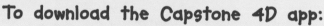

Videos for all of the sidebars in this book
are at your fingertips with the 4D app.

To download the Capstone 4D app:
- Search in the Apple App Store
  or Google Play for "Capstone 4D"
- Click Install (Android) or Get, then Install (Apple)
- Open the application
- Scan any page with this icon

You can also access the additional resources on
the web at www.capstone4D.com using the password
pearl.light

CURIOUS PEARL
SCIENCE GIRL

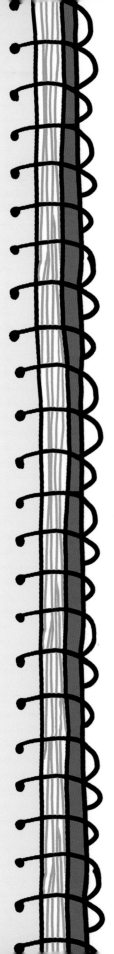

I'm so excited! Sabina and her grandma invited me to their cabin for the weekend. For two days we'll be swimming in the lake and playing in the woods! Our friend Sal got to come too. Sabina, Sal, and me — three best buds.

You know what's even cooler? Sabina brought her water rocket. Look at that thing go!

"Wait, where did the rocket go?" I asked.

"I think it landed by the water," Sal said.

"Let's find it," Sabina said.

When we started searching, Sabina found something — but not the rocket. Her goggles.

"I've been looking everywhere for these," she said. "I can't believe I didn't see them last night. They were right here."

"Well," Sal said, "the Sun is out now."

"What does that have to do with it?" Sabina said.

"The Sun is a big light," Sal said.

"Actually, the Sun makes light," I said. "Light is a form of energy that plants and many animals need."

I stopped and pulled out my notebook. I wanted to write this down.

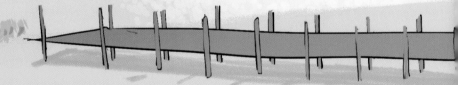

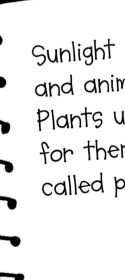

Sunlight is energy that plants and animals need to survive. Plants use sunlight to make food for themselves. The process is called photosynthesis.

"The Sun is the largest source of light," I said. "But there are other sources, like fire and electric lamps."

"Wow, are you a smarty-pants?" Sabina asked.

"I read about it in a book," I said. "I also read that light travels in a straight line. But I don't really understand that. Maybe I'm not a smarty-pants."

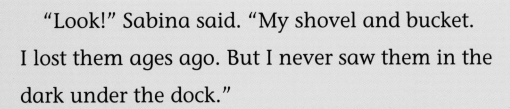

"Look!" Sabina said. "My shovel and bucket. I lost them ages ago. But I never saw them in the dark under the dock."

"Wait," Sal said. "Dark under the dock? When it's light out?"

"The dock's shadow makes it dark underneath," I said.

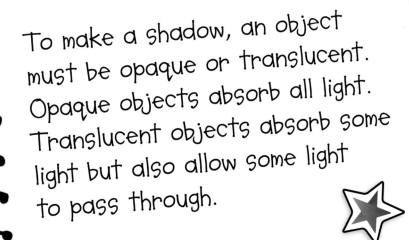

To make a shadow, an object must be opaque or translucent. Opaque objects absorb all light. Translucent objects absorb some light but also allow some light to pass through.

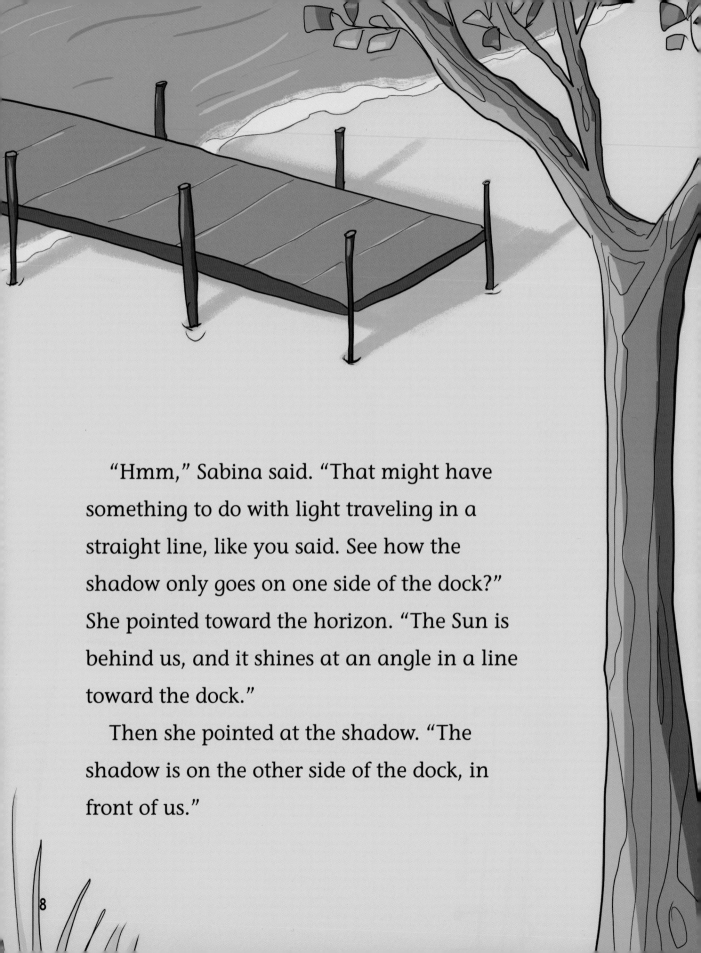

"Hmm," Sabina said. "That might have something to do with light traveling in a straight line, like you said. See how the shadow only goes on one side of the dock?" She pointed toward the horizon. "The Sun is behind us, and it shines at an angle in a line toward the dock."

Then she pointed at the shadow. "The shadow is on the other side of the dock, in front of us."

"Good thinking, Sabina," I said. "Now who's the smarty-pants?"

Before she could answer, Sal pointed and asked, "Hey, what's that?"

We all ran over to see what he was pointing at. It was an old metal box.

"That's my uncle's tackle box," Sabina
said. She held it up to get a better look in
the sunlight.

"Hey, stop that!" Sal said.

"What?" Sabina asked.

"The Sun is reflecting off of the metal, and
it's hitting my eyes," replied Sal. "It hurts."

"I think we're learning something new about light," I said. "When the Sun hits the dock, it stops. But when it hits the metal box, it reflects back." I wrote in my science notebook.

Light reflects off some materials, such as metal or mirrors.

"Time for dinner!" Sabina's grandma said.

We all ran over to the table and sat down.

"Look," Sal said, pointing at my glass.
"The light goes right through your water."

"You're right," I said.

I reached into my bag and grabbed my
magnifying glass. I held it out so the Sun
shone through it.

"Eureka!" I said. "The light goes through the glass too, but it bends. See where the light is hitting the ground?"

"Cool!" said Sal.

"The magnifying glass is transparent," said Sabina's grandma. "That means light shines through it. The bending of light is called refraction."

"Wow," I said, "that makes sense."

Later that evening, we went back outside.

"We'll never find the rocket in the dark," Sal said.

"We can if we bring lights," Sabina said. She handed us both a flashlight.

Just then, I saw something orange in the grass. "A Frisbee!" I said. "Frisbees are plastic. They're translucent. That means some light shines through it."

"Yes, I can see it," Sal replied. "What else is translucent?"

We all brainstormed, and I wrote down some examples.

Thin plastic, paper, and frosted glass are translucent.

I picked up the Frisbee. Sabina shined her
light through it.

"In the light, the Frisbee is bright orange,"
Sabina said. "But when I take the light away,
you can barely tell what color it is."

"My book said that all colors are contained
in light," I said.

Sabina made a funny face. "That makes zero sense," she said.

"It makes perfect sense," her grandma said. "When light hits an object, the object absorbs some of the light. Then you can't see that part of the light. But it also reflects some of the light. Reflected light is the color you see with your eyes."

"I think I get it," I said. "What about something that is white?"

"When something is white, it is reflecting all the colors," she said.

"Now, what do you think is happening when you see black?" Sabina's grandma pointed to the black barbecue grill.

"I have a guess," Sal said. "That object absorbs all the colors and reflects none of them."

"You got it! Smarty-pants!" Sabina's grandma said, smiling.

"Sabina," Sal said. "I think I see your rocket."

We followed him into the tall grass by the water. Yep, there it was. Sabina quickly pumped it up.

I said, "I think you should wait until —"

WHOOOOOOOOOOOSH!

There it went. And went. And . . .

Lost.

Again.

"Let's look for it in the morning," I suggested. "When the Sun is out."

SCIENCE ACTIVITY

Make a Rainbow!

Do you want to see all the colors in light at once? You probably have seen this before. That's what a rainbow is. When light shines through water, the water bends the light and breaks it up into colors.

Here's what you need:

- small mirror that will fit inside the glass
- clear glass filled halfway with water
- sunshine
- sheet of white paper

Steps:

1. Put the mirror into the glass of water.

2. Turn the glass so the mirror faces the Sun, and the Sun shines on it.

3. Hold the sheet of paper in front of the glass so the light reflecting off the mirror hits it.

Check out the rainbow! You can move the paper around to change the shape or position of the rainbow.

GLOSSARY

absorb—to take something in

energy—the ability to do work, such as moving things or giving off heat or light

opaque—not see-through; blocking all rays of light

photosynthesis—a process in which plants use sunlight to make food and oxygen

reflect—to return light from an object

refraction—the bending of light; light is refracted when it travels through a prism or a lens

shadow—a dark shape made by something blocking out light

translucent—letting some light pass through, but not transparent; frosted and stained glass are translucent

transparent—letting light through

READ MORE

Braun, Eric. *Lookin' for Light: Science Adventures with Manny the Origami Moth.* Origami Science Adventures. North Mankato, Minn.: Capstone Press, 2014.

Robin Johnson. *What Are Light Waves?* Light and Sound Waves Close-Up. New York: Crabtree, 2014.

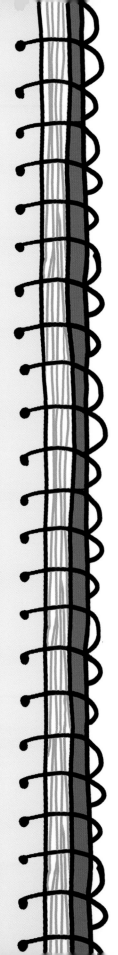

INTERNET SITES

Use FactHound to find Internet sites related to this book.

Visit *www.facthound.com*

Just type in 9781515813453 and go.

CRITICAL THINKING QUESTIONS

What are the different things that can happen to light when it hits an object?

What would the world be like if we had no Sun?

Why do you think most people are active during the day and asleep when it's dark?

MORE BOOKS IN THE SERIES

INDEX

Thanks to our adviser for his expertise, research, and advice:
Christopher T. Ruhland, PhD
Professor of Biological Sciences
Department of Biology
Minnesota State University, Mankato

Editor: Shelly Lyons
Designer: Ted Williams
Art Director: Nathan Gassman
Production Specialist: Katy LaVigne
The illustrations in this book were digitally produced.

Picture Window Books are published by Capstone, 1710 Roe Crest Drive, North Mankato, Minnesota 56003
www.mycapstone.com

Library of Congress Cataloging-in-Publication Data
Cataloging-in-Publication information is on file with Library of Congress.
Names: Braun, Eric, author. | Dehennin, Stephanie, illustrator.
Title: Curious Pearl Investigates Light: 4D An Augmented Reality Science Experience
ISBN 978-1-5158-1345-3 (library binding)
ISBN 978-1-5158-1349-1 (paperback)
ISBN 978-1-5158-1361-3 (eBook PDF)

Printed and bound in the USA.
010373F17